Borderline Personality Disorder

A Complete Guide to the Signs, Symptoms, and Treatment Methods of Borderline Personality Disorder

Table of Contents

Introduction 1

Chapter 1: Understanding Borderline Personality Disorder 2

Chapter 2: Psychotherapy for Borderline Personality Disorder 8

Chapter 3: Medications for Borderline Personality Disorder 15

Chapter 4: Herbal Remedies and Supplements for Borderline Personality Disorder 20

Chapter 5: Rehabilitation and Hospitalization for Borderline Personality Disorder 24

Chapter 6: Disorders that are Similar to BPD 27

Chapter 7: How to Tell your Friends, Family and Colleagues About BPD 30

Chapter 8: How to Help a Loved One with BPD 35

Chapter 9: Holistic Treatment Options 39

Chapter 10: Can you Overcome Borderline Personality Disorder? 42

Chapter 11: Self-Help Strategies 44

Chapter 12: Where to Go for Help/Diagnosis 48

Conclusion 50

Introduction

I want to thank you and congratulate you for picking up the book, "Borderline Personality Disorder".

This is the newly released, 2nd edition of this book, updated with new information, making this book a true complete guide to borderline personality disorder!

This book contains helpful information about borderline personality disorder, the signs and symptoms, and its possible treatments.

Borderline personality disorder is often misunderstood, or misdiagnosed. Surprisingly, not a lot of people know about this disorder, despite it being quite prevalent in society.

You will soon learn how borderline personality disorder is diagnosed, and how it differs from other personality disorders.

This book will provide you the steps and strategies required to successfully understand and manage borderline personality disorder. If you're reading this on behalf of a loved one, this book will also provide you with strategies for communicating with them and helping them with their condition.

Provided within this guide are comprehensive lists of medical, psychological, and self-help strategies for managing and improving borderline personality disorder symptoms.

With the help of this book you'll be well on your way to improving your borderline personality disorder for good!

Thanks again for taking the time to read this book, I hope you find it to be helpful!

Chapter 1:
Understanding Borderline Personality Disorder

Borderline personality disorder is a type of personality disorder characterized by consistently troubling ways of feeling, interacting, and thinking. Negative self-image, abandonment issues, and impulsivity also characterize the disorder. Because of these symptoms, people with borderline personality disorder tend to have a hard time maintaining interpersonal relationships.

Historically, this condition was been believed to be a set of symptoms that included distortions of reality and mood problems. It was thought to be on the borderline between schizophrenia and mood problems. However, it has been learned that even though its symptoms may straddle such complexes, it is still more closely associated with other personality disorders when it comes to its development.

Borderline personality disorder can affect both men and women, although women are more likely to have it than men. Those who suffer from it usually have had traumatizing or distressing experiences as a child. Like many other mental illnesses, experts consider it the result of biological vulnerabilities, social stressors, and ways of thinking. Other types of disorders tend to occur along with it.

For instance, men with borderline personality disorder also tend to have addiction problems while women with the same condition tend to have eating disorders. In adolescents, it can also co-occur with odd personality and anxiety disorders, such as passive aggressive personality disorder and schizophrenia.

Adults with antisocial personality disorder are also likely to have borderline personality disorder.

In the past, there has been a controversy as to whether or not borderline personality disorder is its own disorder or simply a variation of bipolar disorder. Eventually, researchers concluded that it is a disorder of its own due to its complex and unique characteristics. Some people with this disorder have it alone. Others, on the other hand, have it along with bipolar or any other mental disorder.

Causes of Borderline Personality Disorder

While there is no specific cause for borderline personality disorder, certain factors are believed to contribute to its development. Among these are biological factors and brain abnormalities. Individuals with the disorder are more likely to have an abnormality with their hippocampus, frontal lobes, and amygdala. Research shows that the areas of their brain associated with aggression, emotion regulation, and impulsivity have changed. Likewise, some of their brain chemicals have been found to stop functioning properly.

Some researchers also claim that the brains of people with borderline personality disorder tend to have areas that are more or less active than the brains of those who do not have the disorder. Environmental factors may have also caused it in some people. According to studies, many people with borderline personality disorder have suffered abuse or have been neglected or separated from parents, loved ones, or caregivers in childhood.

Another perceived cause for this disorder is genetics. According to some studies of families and twins, personality disorders are hereditary. They also have a close connection to other mental disorders within family members. Psychologically, borderline personality disorder seems to make an individual more prone to experiencing stress when it comes to dealing with emotions. Socially, it predisposes those who have it to be more likely to expect rejection and criticism.

Risk Factors

People who grew up experiencing or witnessing substance abuse, sexual abuse, neglect, death, or divorce, in their families have a higher risk of developing borderline personality disorder. Adolescents with addiction or alcohol abuse are also very likely to have it. Moreover, children with certain temperaments or learning problems can also be at risk of developing this disorder.

Symptoms of Borderline Personality Disorder

Individuals with borderline personality disorder tend to exhibit impulsive behaviors and other symptoms, including frantic avoidance of imagined, or real, abandonment. Such perception of an impending rejection or separation can cause them to experience changes in their emotions, behavior, self-image, and thinking. They become highly sensitive to everything that goes on around them.

In addition, they harbor intense feelings of anger and a fear of abandonment, even when they face realistic separation or an unavoidable change of plans. For instance, they can get very angry when someone cancels or is late for a meeting, even if it is only by a few minutes. They may also believe that such abandonment means that they are bad or not good enough.

Oftentimes, the fears of abandonment that these people feel are linked to a need for other people to be around them or an intolerance of being alone. The frantic efforts that they exert to avoid the risk of being abandoned may include impulsive actions, such as suicidal tendencies or self-mutilation.

Another common symptom that people with borderline personality disorder show is a pattern of intense and unstable interpersonal relationships, typically characterized by alternating between extremes of devaluation and idealization. These people have a tendency to idealize potential lovers or caregivers at the first meeting.

Early on in their relationship, they tend to share very intimate details and demand to spend a lot of time together. Then, they quickly switch from idealizing to devaluing their partner. They start to feel that the other person does not give or care enough. They may seem to nurture and empathize with other people, but only if they will never leave them.

People with borderline personality disorder want other people to meet their demands and needs. They are prone to dramatic and sudden shifts in emotions. They may see other people as either cruel or supportive. They may also harbor disillusions with their caregivers who either nurtured or abandoned them.

Identity disturbance is another common symptom of borderline personality disorder. People with this disorder tend to have a persistent and significant unstable sense of self or self-image. They tend to shift aspirations and goals suddenly and dramatically. They may also change their plans and opinions about their values, sexual identity, career, and even types of friends.

They may also suddenly change from being a needy person to an avenger. Even though they have a self-image based on being evil or bad, they may also have feelings that do not really exist. For instance, if they face a situation wherein they feel a lack of support, they may not give their best performance.

Furthermore, people with borderline personality disorder tend to show impulsivity in areas that may be self-damaging. They may be impulsive shoppers, reckless drivers, binge eaters, or substance addicts. They may also display recurrent suicidal behavior, as well as threats and self-mutilating behavior.

Due to their mood swings, they may also have emotional instability. At any one point, they may experience irritability. Eventually, that can turn into anxiety or episodic dysphoria. Such mood swings may last for a few hours or days. They may also have chronic feelings of emptiness, as well as intense anger that are no longer appropriate.

People with borderline personality disorder can get angry even when there is really nothing to get angry about. They may also have a hard time controlling or managing their anger issues. Furthermore, they may show transient and stress-related paranoid thoughts.

Borderline personality disorder involves enduring and long-standing patterns of behavior usually diagnosed in adulthood. Children and adolescents are usually not diagnosed with the disorder due to the constant changes in their personality and behavior.

Nonetheless, a child or an adolescent may still be diagnosed with the disorder if they have been exhibiting symptoms for a year or more. Adults, on the other hand, are expected to have fewer and less intense symptoms, as they get older. However, those who are in their 40s and 50s are expected to experience the most intense symptoms.

Diagnosis of Borderline Personality Disorder

A psychologist, psychiatrist or any other trained mental health professional can diagnose personality disorders, including borderline personality disorder. General practitioners and family physicians are generally not well-equipped or trained to diagnose a person with personality disorder.

The diagnosis of borderline personality disorder involves having a series of tests and comparing symptoms. Patients are also asked about their medical history and family history. As you have learned earlier, personality disorder may be linked to genetics. People with family members who have personality disorders are also prone to having them.

Chapter 2:
Psychotherapy for Borderline Personality Disorder

Also known as talk therapy, psychotherapy is a treatment approach that involves a variety of types, such as dialectical behavior therapy, cognitive behavioral therapy, mentalization-based therapy, schema-focused therapy, and transference-focused psychotherapy.

Like with any other personality disorder, psychotherapy is commonly used to treat patients to help them overcome their problem. It is important to take note that even though medications can be effective solutions for symptoms, they may have unpleasant side effects.

In addition, medications cannot help patients learn emotion regulation, coping skills, and other important skills that they can use to improve their life. In addition, a major objective of psychotherapy is to prevent a person with a personality disorder from committing suicide.

It is crucial to assess and monitor the tendency to become suicidal all throughout the whole course of treatment. When a person with borderline personality disorder displays severe symptoms, they may need to receive medication or even undergo hospitalization.

The following types of psychotherapy should be tried first, before choosing a more invasive treatment procedure.

Cognitive Behavioral Therapy

Cognitive behavioral therapy involves working with a mental health counselor to become more aware of negative, ineffective, and inaccurate thinking. Patients also work with a therapist so they can see challenging situations more objectively and clearly. In addition, they work with a therapist so they can learn how to practice alternative solution techniques.

What can you expect from it? Well, cognitive behavior therapy focuses mainly on the present moment. This means that you should not dwell on your past experiences. You are still allowed to explain how you came to behave or think the way you do, but you should focus on how you think and act at the present.

Cognitive behavior therapy is also directive. You can expect the therapist to be active during every session. He/she will give you direct advice. In other therapies, the therapists mostly sit back and listen while the patients direct the session.

In addition, in cognitive behavioral therapy, the therapists generally assume that your symptoms are associated with the behavior and thinking patterns that you have adapted throughout the years. Hence, they do not believe that simply spending one to two hours per week in therapy is enough to produce significant results.

They are most likely to give homework and let the patients work on changing their behavior and thinking patterns outside of therapy sessions. Before a session ends, homework sheets and handouts are usually given.

Dialectical Behavior Therapy

Dialectical behavior therapy is especially designed to treat borderline personality disorder. In general, it is done through phone counseling, individual sessions, and group sessions. It makes use of a skills-based approach combined with meditation and physical exercises to help patients learn how to regulate their emotions, improve relationships, and tolerate distress.

During individual therapy, the individual therapist is the main therapist and the patient undergoes individual therapy sessions. The patient goes to the office of the therapist to talk about their thoughts and feelings among other things.

During telephone contact, the patient speaks to the therapist via telephone in between therapy sessions. However, it is important to note that telephone contact is not done for the purpose of psychotherapy. Instead, it provides the patient the support and help that they need to apply the skills that they have learned to real life situations, as well as to help them avoid injuring themselves.

The patient may also call their therapist if they want to mend any issues between them prior to the next therapy session. However, they're not allowed to call within the next twenty-four hours if they injure themselves. This is to avoid the reinforcement of self-injury.

In skills training, a patient speaks with a therapist along with a group of people with the same condition. These patients are taught skills that may be useful to their daily situations. These skills include core mindfulness skills, emotion modulation skills, interpersonal effectiveness skills, and distress tolerance skills.

Core mindfulness skills are based on certain Buddhist meditation techniques, but without any religious allegiance involved. Such techniques are used to enable the patients to be more aware of their experiences, as well as to develop the ability to be mindful of the present moment.

Interpersonal effectiveness skills focus on achieving one's goals with other people. The patients are taught how to ask for what they want, refuse requests or offers, maintain good relationships with other people, and improve their self-esteem.

Emotion modulation skills are about ways to change distressing emotional states. Distress tolerance skills, on the other hand, include techniques for dealing with such emotional states if it is not possible for them to be changed.

In therapist consultation groups, the therapists receive dialectical behavior therapy from one another. The members of the group have to stay focused. They are also required to give a formal undertaking to stay in dialectical behavior therapy mode and avoid making pejorative remarks against the other members.

Schema-Focused Therapy

Schema-focused therapy combines different approaches of therapies, particularly emotion-based techniques and cognitive behavior therapy, to help patients evaluate repetitive life themes and life patterns so they can identify positive patterns and correct negative ones. It focuses on helping them change negative and long-standing self-images through letter writing, role-playing, anger management, assertiveness training, relaxation, guided imagery, and gradual exposure to situations that induce anxiety.

Limited re-parenting is one unique key element of schema-focused therapy. Here, the patients are able to establish a secure attachment to their therapist. This is, of course, within the bounds of a professional relationship. According to Dr. Joan Farrell, director of the Schema Therapy Institute Midwest Indianapolis Center, many people with borderline personality disorder missed emotional learning when they were younger. They were not encouraged to express their needs and emotions.

They also did not receive adequate validation, which is why their core childhood needs are met in schema therapy. Their therapist ensures that such needs are met by expressing compassion, providing nurturance, and setting limitations. After the therapy, patients are expected to become healthy emotionally. They are also expected to be autonomous enough so they will no longer need their therapist to meet their core needs. Instead, they should be able to meet such needs on their own.

Mentalization-Based Therapy

Mentalization-based therapy is a type of psychodynamically-oriented psychotherapy that helps patients identify and isolate their feelings and thoughts from those of other people. It mainly focuses on thinking before reacting. Patients who undergo this treatment are taught how to separate their feelings and thoughts from the feelings and thoughts of other people.

Individuals with borderline personality disorder usually have intense and unstable relationships that cause them to manipulate or exploit other people unconsciously. They are not able to recognize the effects of their behavior on other people. Through, mentalization, they can learn how to understand feelings and behavior, as well as associate these elements with specific mental states.

According to research, individuals with borderline personality disorder do not have a high capacity for mentalization. You should take note that mentalization is a crucial component in traditional psychotherapy. In mentalization-based therapy, its concept is emphasized, practiced and reinforced within a supportive and safe psychotherapy setting. Mentalization-based therapy is less directive than cognitive behavior therapy.

Transference-Focused Psychotherapy

Transference-focused psychotherapy is also commonly referred to as psychodynamic psychotherapy. It aims to help patients understand their interpersonal and emotional difficulties through the development of relationships between them and their therapists. One of its most distinguishable features is its emphasis on the psychological structure that underlies the symptoms of borderline personality disorder.

Transference-focused psychotherapy also focuses on a deep psychological setup in which the mind is structured around a fundamental split that identifies a way of experiencing oneself and ones surroundings. Such a split determines the perceptions of the patient and results in impulsive self-destructive behaviors and chaotic interpersonal relations. It was actually based on a model of the mind wherein early affectively charged experiences have been established in the psychological structure of the patient.

When you undergo this treatment, you will be taught how to apply your insights into real situations. Your beliefs, attitudes, and internal images will be transferred onto your therapist. By examining this transference, you will be able to work through the distorted images that you automatically impose on external reality. Over time, your capacity for self-reflection will increase and you will be able to adapt to life better.

Conversely, your symptoms of borderline personality disorder will decrease.

Every patient needs to be in a structured therapeutic setting, no matter what type of therapy he or she goes through. Individuals with borderline personality disorder usually try to test the limitations of their therapist during treatment. Hence, it is important to establish a well-defined and proper boundary at the beginning of the therapy session.

Clinicians should be aware of their feelings towards their patients, especially when the latter start to show inappropriate behaviors. People with this type of personality disorder tend to be discriminated against unfairly because others see them as troublemakers. A lot of people do not understand the true nature of their condition, which is why they are often shunned.

Dr. Phillip Long notes that these patients may actually need more care than other patients and that their rowdy behavior may only be caused by their personality disorder. He also notes that a therapeutic alliance must develop within the treatment and experiences of the patient with their therapist.

Moreover, the therapists should be tolerant despite repeated episodes of rage, fear, and distrust of their patients. They should also avoid uncovering to boost ego defenses, so the patients can be less anxious about loss and fragmentation. The main goals of therapy must not be in terms of complete personality restructuring, but rather in terms of life gains towards independent functioning.

Chapter 3: Medications for Borderline Personality Disorder

Various medications are available to treat clinical problems that are associated with borderline personality disorder. Such problems include depression, anxiety, and impulsiveness. According to Dr. Phillip Long, low dosages of antipsychotic medications can be beneficial during brief reactive psychoses. However, such medications are usually not helpful to the treatment regimen because episodes tend to be short-term and self-limiting.

Nevertheless, it has been found that low dosages of high potency neuroleptics, such as haloperidol, can organize thought patterns and treat certain psychotic symptoms. In some cases, neuroleptics can also treat depression. Such medications are especially recommended for patients who display uncontrollable anger issues. Then again, these should be given in low dosages and only with psychosocial intervention. They may also not be advisable for long-term usage due to their side effects.

Antidepressants

Antidepressants are typically recommended to people with comorbid depression. Nonetheless, they are also useful in treating patients with borderline personality disorder. Those who show signs of suicidal intent and ideation are most commonly given a prescription of these drugs.

There are different types of antidepressants. Selective serotonin reuptake inhibitors (SSRIs) are the most common. They work by changing the availability of serotonin, a neurotransmitter, in the brain. Citalopram, escitalopram, fluoxetine, paroxetine, and sertraline are some examples of SSRIs.

Other types of commonly prescribed antidepressants are tricyclics and monoamine oxidase inhibitors (MAOIs). Examples of tricyclics include amitriptyline, clomipramine, and imipramine. MAOIs are older types of antidepressants and are rarely prescribed due to their severe side effects. Examples of MAOIs include phenelzine and tranylcypromine.

Several studies show that antidepressants are effective in treating the symptoms of borderline personality disorder. SSRIs, for instance, can reduce anger, emotional instability, self-harm tendencies, and impulsivity. MAOIs are also effective in reducing emotional instability.

As for the side effects and risks of antidepressants, they may vary depending on their type. If you are taking SSRIs, you may experience a loss of appetite, insomnia, headaches, sexual dysfunction, and sedation. If you are taking tricyclics, you may experience dry mouth, weight gain, blurred vision, heart problems, and seizures.

If you are on MAOIs, you should avoid consuming certain food products. Soy sauce, cheese, and foods that contain high amounts of tyramine, an amino acid, can increase your risk of severe high blood pressure. If you are taking other medications, MAOIs may also interfere with their effectiveness.

Anti-Anxiety Drugs

Anti-anxiety drugs, also known as anxiolytics, can treat the intense agitation and anxiety that come with borderline personality disorder. Several studies have shown that these medications are effective in reducing its symptoms. However, there is no controlled clinical trial yet that examines the usefulness of these medications for the disorder.

The most commonly used anti-anxiety drugs are benzodiazepines. These include diazepam, alprazolam, lorazepam, and clonazepam. It should be noted that these drugs could be habit-forming. Hence, they are not ideal for people who also have substance addiction problems aside from borderline personality disorder. They may just use non-benzodiazepine for anxiety instead.

In addition, avoid taking benzodiazepines with alcohol or other sedating medications. Otherwise, they can have severe side effects. Some of the common side effects of anti-anxiety medications are fatigue, sleepiness, memory problems, and impaired coordination.

Antipsychotics

According to research, antipsychotics can effectively reduce paranoid thinking, anxiety, impulsivity, hostility, and anger in people with borderline personality disorder. These drugs have two main types: atypical and typical.

Typical antipsychotics are the older generation of antipsychotics. Because of this, they are rarely used. They are also not recommended for long-term use due to their serious side effects. Some examples of typical antipsychotics are haloperidol, thioridazine, chlorpromazine, and fluphenazine.

Atypical antipsychothics, on the other hand, are the newer generation of antipsychotics. Some examples include olanzapine, clozapine, quetiapine, aripiprazole, and risperidone. These drugs generally have less movement-related side effects such as tardive dyskinesia and akathisia.

Tardive dyskinesia is a side effect that occurs when antipsychotics are used for the long term. It involves uncontrollable movements of the limbs, fingers, tongue, lips, and face. Akathisia is another known side effect of long-term usage of antipsychotics. It involves intense agitation and restlessness.

Nonetheless, other common side effects of antipsychotics include dry mouth, weight gain, sedation, and sexual dysfunction. Clozapine may also cause agranulocytosis, which is a reduction of white blood cells. Neuroleptic malignant syndrome may also occur. This serious condition involves a high fever, muscle rigidity, and delirium.

Mood Stabilizers

Mood stabilizers are medications that reduce intense mood shifts. They can reduce the impulsivity symptoms and emotion dysregulation that come with borderline personality disorder.

Anticonvulsants, drugs that are used to treat seizures, also contain mood-stabilizing properties. Some examples are carbamazepine, lamotrigine, topiramate, oxcarbazepine, valproic acid, and divalproex sodium. Non-convulsant mood stabilizers, such as lithium carbonate, are also commonly used to treat mental disorders.

The side effects and risks associated with mood stabilizers may vary depending on their type. For instance, lithium carbonate may cause weight gain, gastrointestinal problems, tremors, cognitive problems, and acne. It can also affect the thyroid gland and kidneys. It can even be toxic when taken in high amounts.

Chapter 4:
Herbal Remedies and Supplements for Borderline Personality Disorder

If you do not want to experience the side effects of medications, you can turn to natural treatments such as herbal remedies. They are less expensive, but can be just as effective as medications for borderline personality disorder. Furthermore, you can take supplements. They contain ingredients that can help you reduce your symptoms.

Herbal Remedies

Yerba Mate

This herb is native to Argentina and can serve as a natural antidepressant, mood stabilizer, and anti-anxiety medication. In fact, it is given to Argentinian children to regulate their temperaments. John Lust, author of the book 'The Herb Book', also says that it is an ideal stimulant. Yerba mate can also provide relief from fatigue, stimulate mental energy, and improve mood.

Kava Kava

This herb is useful in fighting anxiety, fatigue, and insomnia. According to the National Center for Complementary and Alternative Medicine, it is effective in treating anxiety disorders. You can use it in place of tricyclics and benzodiazepines because it does not interfere with mental alertness.

However, it has side effects such as liver damage. Experts generally do not recommend people to take this herbal remedy for more than three months. It is not also advisable to take this with psychotropic medications.

Valerian

Lo Ha Wa Ti An Ka, a traditional Osage healer, calls this herb Grandmother Earth's Valium and uses it as a nerve tonic. Since the early years, people have used valerian to treat insomnia, depression, and anxiety. It is effective in relieving tension, pain, and excessive strain. It also soothes the nervous system and brain.

However, it is not advisable to take this herb with sleeping medications because it can interfere with their effectiveness. It can also cause hallucinations. Individuals with borderline personality disorder can take it in low dosages with two- to three-week breaks in between. They can also blend it with tea.

Chamomile

Chamomile is popular for its soothing properties. It can significantly boost your mood. You can take it in the form of a tea.

St. John's Wort

St. John's Wort works by blocking the ability of your body to absorb serotonin, thus increasing its levels. This herb is perhaps the most popular herb for enhancing mood and reducing symptoms of various mental disorders. Numerous studies have found that it can be just as effective as antidepressants when it comes to treating anxiety and depression. Then again, you should avoid taking it with SSRIs, MAOIs, and supplements because it can affect your production of serotonin.

Supplements

S-Adenosyl L-Methionine (SAM-e)

This amino acid is naturally found in your body. It plays a huge role in the production of mood enhancing neurotransmitters, such as dopamine and serotonin. Multiple clinical trials and studies show that it can reduce your symptoms of depression. If you do not have sufficient amounts of SAM-e, you may be in a bad mood.

If you have just started taking SAM-e, see to it that you start with low dosages. Keep in mind that the higher the dosage, the greater the risk of a manic episode. In addition, you should take note that it can cause insomnia. Therefore, you need to take it in the morning on an empty stomach. For best results, you should also take B vitamins.

5-Hydroxytryptophan (5-HTP)

Just like SAM-e, 5-HTP is naturally found in the body. It works by regulating and increasing your production of serotonin. As a result, you become less depressed or anxious. You are also able to fight insomnia and sleep better at night. Initially, you should take this medication at fifty milligrams or below. Gradually, you should increase the amount up to one hundred milligrams.

Docosahexaenoic Acid (DHA)

This omega-3 fatty acid is usually present in cold-water oceanic fish oils. According to research, it works in the same manner as Lithium, but without the severe side effects. You can take DHA in the form of capsules. Just make sure that you read their labels carefully to find out if it contains low DHA levels and high EPA levels. Ideally, you should take one hundred to two hundred milligrams of DHA per day.

Chapter 5:
Rehabilitation and Hospitalization for Borderline Personality Disorder

Borderline personality disorder can make your everyday living difficult if you cannot control your symptoms. Although you can resort to medications, herbal remedies, and other alternative treatments, you may still not be able to fully function in society. If you find yourself being uncontrollable or experiencing extreme symptoms, you should consider checking into a rehabilitation facility or hospital.

Rehabilitation

If you think that you need more than therapy alone, you can enter a rehabilitation facility and stay there for three to four months, or until you get better. There are plenty of rehabilitation centers for borderline personality disorder and other mental illnesses all over the United States. Each one has its own set of rules or policies.

Most of these rehabilitation facilities conduct psychological testing to clarify diagnoses, identify the needs of the patients, and provide further information about their individualized treatment plan. Psychological testing may also be necessary if a patient has had a traumatic brain injury or has special needs.

Every patient is evaluated based on a set of personality traits and cognitive abilities. Their intelligence is also measured through psychological testing. They are evaluated based on verbal skills, problem solving or reasoning skills, speed processing, and basic memory skills.

Likewise, specific memory abilities are also evaluated. These include long-term memory, short-term memory, memory for information seen, and memory for information heard. Their abilities in reading, math, spelling, and comprehension are also assessed in order to find out if they have any learning disability.

Rehabilitation also identifies personality traits. The patient undergoes tests to find out if their personality traits affect their functioning in a positive or negative manner. Furthermore, they undergo tests that can accurately determine their diagnosis as well as understand what areas affect their mental health. Additional tests to understand neurological issues, motivational issues, or potential thought disorders are also available.

Hospitalization

Hospitalization may be the last resort for a person with borderline personality disorder. Many people are actually hesitant to be confined in a hospital. However, when their disorder is no longer treatable with just medication and therapy alone, they may need to undergo treatments in a hospital facility.

If things get out of control, they can be a hazard to themselves, their families, their therapists, and their communities. Some patients are admitted to emergency rooms as a form of immediate crisis intervention. However, this may not be the best idea because it can be very expensive.

Instead, patients are encouraged to find social support within their community. For instance, they may join self-help support groups or contact a crisis hotline. Emergency room staff are not encouraged to treat patients in blind conjunction with other doctors or therapists who are treating the patient at another facility.

They have to contact the primary therapist or attending physician of their patients before they administer medication. Crisis management of immediate problems is also a vital component in the effective treatment of borderline personality disorder.

Chapter 6:
Disorders that are Similar to BPD

There are some disorders out there that may be confused with BPD. After all, feelings of anxiousness can be seen in many personality and mental disorders. Negative thinking is the same. Below are some disorders that are similar to Borderline Personality Disorder that may be confused with BPD at times.

Anxiety Disorders

Generalized Anxiety Disorder (GAD) is similar to BPD in such a way that the afflicted person is controlled by a terrible feeling of anxiety. The person worries about intangible things instead of something specific. Their fears can also be so intense that they can potentially take over the person's life.

There are many other types of anxieties, but the rest are more specific – often understandable, but still intense. An example of such is separation anxiety disorder. While it may be understandable for a mom whose child is going to school for the first time to be anxious, being crippled with this anxiety is no longer normal.

Alcoholism

A problem that can occur together with BPD is alcoholism. A person who is suffering from BPD may indulge in alcohol abuse. Inebriation, for them, can be the answer to tempering their feelings of self-doubt and social anxiety. Alcoholism can develop due to many reasons, but it can develop from a desire to alleviate feelings of anxiety.

Antisocial personality disorder

Like BPD, antisocial personality disorder is characterized by impulsive behavior. What makes it different, however, is that an antisocial person is prone to aggression and a total disregard for other person's feelings and safety. Such a person is not interested in the safety of others and has trouble empathizing with other people, in other words putting oneself in the situation of other people. Because of this lack of empathy, the antisocial person commits acts against others with a lack of remorse.

Bipolar disorder

This disorder has been put under the spotlight lately due to several celebrities' admission to being sufferers. Bipolar people have manic periods where they may be excitable, risky, and full of energy, followed by periods of depression and anxiety.

Eating disorders

Like BPD sufferers, people with eating disorders have poor body image. Bulimics and anorexics view themselves in a very different way. Some claim to literally see themselves as fat when they look in the mirror, even though they are clearly anorexic to everyone else. Such a disorder is called body dysmorphic disorder, which is beyond merely having a poor body image or poor self-confidence.

Histrionic personality disorder

A person with histrionic personality disorder may appear to be the opposite of those with BPD or antisocial personality disorder because of their desire to be in the thick of things. Histrionics tend to exaggerate their feelings, reactions, and stories in order to be the center of attention. Like those with BPD and antisocial personality disorder, they are willing to take risks. However, these risks are motivated by their desire to be noticed. Though histrionics seem to be very different from those with BPD because of their apparent extroversion, their inability to interact normally with other people makes them similar to those with BPD.

Narcissistic personality disorder

Narcissistic people are somewhat similar to histrionics. They want to be noticed and they believe that they should be noticed. However, their massive self-importance may make them seem arrogant to others; thus, causing a problem when it comes to interpersonal relations. So, narcissists do have something in common with BPD sufferers: their difficulty in interacting with other people.

The above disorders have their similarities and differences. However, all of them are similar to BPD in the sense that they affect how a person interacts with other people.

Chapter 7:
How to Tell your Friends, Family and Colleagues About BPD

There are two main reasons for telling someone about borderline personality disorder: 1) you think that person has BPD, and 2) you think you have BPD and want your family to know about it. So, talking about it may put you on one side or the other, unless you are a therapist, a professor, or someone who has a special interest in the personality disorder.

How to tell someone you think they may have BPD

It is going to be difficult. Remember that someone who has BPD has problems with normally interacting with other people. They will be immediately distressed when they believe someone is criticizing them or telling them something that they do not want to hear. If you do not tell that person the right way, you may lose the chance of telling them at all.

Use an emphatic approach

When approaching a person with BPD, you have to make sure that you are using an understanding tone. Let him/her know that you know what they're feeling. Tell them that while you don't necessarily like their behavior, that you understand what they are going through. Use a calm voice, and be gentle in your approach.

Cite examples from experience

Talk about instances where the person's behavior has confused you. Do not be confrontational. Try to stay logical even if the memories may distress you. Try to show the discrepancies in the person's behavior and how they may have made some abrupt and unexplainable changes in mood, decisions and the things that they have said. Tell them that you just want to understand what is going on and that you are in no way trying to mock or anger them.

Propose your willingness to support

Show the person that you are willing to support them if they choose to seek help. You will be there to provide emotional support if they need you to be there. Remember that you are talking to a colleague, friend or a family member. You want the best for them. Remember that they're going through something that they could not help.

Expect resistance and interpret it accordingly

It won't be easy. It won't be smooth. Most likely, you will meet resistance. If you see that the other person is distressed or is outwardly fighting, stop. This means to say that the time is not yet right.

Don't be surprised if the BPD sufferer looks at you as if you are a traitor or as if you are the one who needs to seek treatment. They may even feel betrayed. If that is the case, then stop pushing. Wait for the person to accept the observations themselves.

Use the right non-verbal cues

Your verbal communication may not be enough. You need to make yourself appear open to communication, and non-threatening. This means to say that you should not have any distractions, such as your phone or the television. You want to get the person's attention while making sure that he/she knows that they have yours.

Your arms should remain uncrossed to signify interest and openness. Sit up straight and do not fidget. Show that you are focused on the person. Keep a neutral face, as well, so that they don't feel like you're judging them.

No matter how good you are at communicating, be prepared for the possibility that your help will get rejected. You should continue looking for new strategies to use in convincing them to get help.

How to tell someone you have BPD

If you are the BPD sufferer and you want to tell someone about your disorder, congratulations – that's a great step. The desire to help yourself is already there. This means that you are closer to treatment than someone who is still in denial about their condition.

Get officially diagnosed first

It is possible that you may have not been clinically diagnosed yet. Before telling someone about it, perhaps it is best to have a talk with a therapist. Get diagnosed officially. This way, you know that you are not just imagining things. After all, there are some personality disorders that are similar to borderline personality disorder. You may have one of them, instead. It is also possible that you do not have any disorder but are just much more stressed recently.

Be sure about your decision

Before you tell anyone about your official diagnosis, you have to be sure about it first. Will you really be comfortable having this person know about it? It's important to seek help and support, but you should choose to get this support from the right people.

Be sure about the person

Having borderline personality disorder is not normally something that people happily announce to the world. However, it is important to seek help and support from those around you. The first instinct will be to tell family members and friends. People who have known you all of your life will be more accepting. If you know them well enough, you will also have an idea as to how they will react when you talk about your diagnosis.

Secure a fact sheet

On your trip to the therapist, ask for a fact sheet. You can share this with people that you are revealing the information to. Talk about the symptoms and the prognosis of the condition so that they will better understand it. The fact sheet will help them understand that there are times when you cannot help your behavior. Do not expect that they will forgive you for your past behavior, but at least, this may help resolve some problems.

Also, talk about possible medications and therapy. Talk to them about any treatment that you are going through. If you are close with them, they will appreciate your efforts to get better.

It does sound easier for a person with bipolar personality disorder to take the first step in a dialogue about the disorder. After all, they have already realized that something is wrong and done something to correct it. It will be harder to try to persuade someone to get checked in the first place. However, it's worthwhile having the conversation if you truly want to help the person.

It can be difficult whether you are talking to people about their condition or if you are talking about your own condition. Borderline personality disorder is difficult to talk about but the topic shouldn't be silenced. There is very little awareness about BPD, and having support structures in place is paramount in managing and improving the disorder.

Chapter 8:
How to Help a Loved One with BPD

The first step when helping someone with BPD is accepting the diagnosis. Do not look upon it with disgust or fear. Instead, convey your full support to your loved one. This support must be clearly shown. People with borderline personality disorder are already having problems with interpersonal relationships. They do not quite know how to adjust to people, so it's best if they have emotional support.

Get the facts about the condition

After you have accepted your loved one's diagnosis or once you begin having the nagging suspicion that they have BPD, it is time to conduct some research. You should know what the symptoms are and what is myth and not fact.

1. BPD sufferers care

You should understand that people with BPD do care. Do not feel as if you are engaging in a one-way traffic type of relationship. Instead, understand that while BPD sufferers may display some strange or even unacceptable behaviors, they do feel remorse about what they have done after they realize what they did.

2. BPD is not a result of poor parenting.

BPD sufferers have been born with the sensitivity that they are displaying. Their condition is not the result of poor parenting, of having been neglected or abused. They have come with the biological predisposition to the condition.

3. BPD sufferers are not necessarily dangerous.

There are people who are dangerous not because they have a personality disorder. They just are. For some reason, they have the capability to harm other individuals. It just so happens that there are also individuals who have either a personality or a mental disorder who are also inclined to harm others. While it is true that some personality disorders reduce one's capability to feel sorry about what they have done, these conditions do not automatically make someone dangerous, so do not be scared of your loved one who has BPD.

4. BPD sufferers do not attempt suicide just to get your attention

Those who are suffering from the potentially will try to end their lives. This is not an attention-seeking act, and needs to be taken seriously. Approximately 8 to 11% of sufferers have attempted suicide.

Know how to handle their condition

With information under your belt, you should be able to handle your loved one with BPD better. Remember to use the right tone and stance when trying to get them to seek help. Do not take a combative stance when communicating with them. They likely feel alone already, so fighting with them will simply make things worse.

BPD sufferers can display all sorts of disturbing symptoms: anxiety, eating disorders, depression and even bipolar disorder. It can occur together with other personality disorders. Your loved one may act out in dangerous and inappropriate ways. They may even be hurtful, doing things that you may ordinarily assume that they are aware of being terrible. They may regret the actions later, but during the moment, they won't be able to empathize with you. Try to not take their actions or words to heart.

It takes some sacrifice to deal with someone with borderline personality disorder. You may feel like you have to protect your own mind and body from harm because you are constantly treading carefully with someone who may always see you as being at fault. A BPD sufferer also experiences extremes of emotion, from extreme giddiness to the lowest depression.

They may even try to manipulate you into doing and feeling things. So, yes, it can be grueling to live with someone with BPD. You have to prepare yourself with all the knowledge you can get so that you will not feel personally affronted each time your loved one does something you deem to be inappropriate or hurtful.

Get help

When your loved one is ready – that is, if they no longer feel threatened and betrayed – seek help for them. You may have already sought help for them even before this step. If they don't accept the reality of their condition at first, you should talk to a therapist in secret. Consult with a professional on how you can best handle the situation at home if your suffering loved one is still not receiving any form of treatment.

Encourage them to get help

To get the best help, encourage your loved one to seek stress relieving therapy. You may also seek the help of a therapist who will focus on your relationship and not just the condition itself. Many relationships have suffered because of borderline personality disorder. While you may be the understanding partner in the relationship, it is also good to be clear that you feel hurt about your loved one's behavior.

When they are focused and listening, tell them calmly about your personal feelings about the matter. You are a human with feelings. Let them recognize this and when they're ready, let them take some responsibility for their actions. It's not completely their fault but they should accept how their actions can take a toll on your emotional health, as well.

Chapter 9:
Holistic Treatment Options

There are many ways through which one can treat borderline personality disorder. It is best, however, to combine several options to help the patient recover in all the aspects of their life. Holistic healing will not only tame the symptoms but also help smooth relationships and interpersonal ties, and the patient's general ability to handle stress.

Relaxation Techniques and Meditation

With borderline personality disorder, relaxation can be a little tricky. The patient's emotions are volatile. They can change from depressed and low, to angry and risk-prone. When angry, the BPD sufferer should be treated with relaxation techniques that can alleviate the symptoms of "fight" that their brain's chemicals are arousing in them. They should then engage in activities that will relax the muscles and mind, such as meditation, deep breathing and guided imagery.

During depressed episodes, it is best to treat the BPD sufferer with massage, rhythmic exercises and yoga that will energize and stimulate the nervous system.

A combination of these relaxation techniques will help the BPD sufferer alleviate their symptoms or at least soothe them enough to make them pause for a while before engaging in risky behavior or saying hurtful things to a loved one.

Relationship Therapy

A good treatment option for those in relationships, or in a family environment is relationship therapy. Before the diagnosis was made, the non-BPD sufferer in the relationship was likely hurt by the actions of the BPD sufferer. The relationship may have been tainted by feelings of betrayal, distrust and resentment.

Through relationship therapy, the BPD sufferer will hopefully learn how to behave more appropriately towards other people. Their friends and family, on the other hand, will learn how to communicate more successfully.

Mindfulness Practice

Mindfulness is about focusing on any given moment. It sounds very simple but it is actually quite difficult to do in this day and age. Everyone is trying his or her best to multitask. Mothers have to work and watch their children at the same time. Employees in the office are expected to deliver their best work on several projects at a time. Students do not only focus on academics but also engage in sports, advanced classes, and other extracurricular activities.

With mindfulness, you literally stop and smell the roses. You breathe in the details of your world as you walk to your office building. You make time to notice the little efforts that your loved ones have made. By looking at life more closely, the BPD sufferer is able to appreciate it better. Mindfulness does not only promote better mental health, but also a better general sense of wellbeing.

Therapy

It is also good for the BPD sufferer to be treated under the guidance of a professional therapist. They will receive guidance in terms of various ways to relieve stress. They can also go through new relaxation techniques with the therapist. The sufferer will learn to understand their condition better, thus providing them with knowledge on things like: what to eat, how to deal with problems, what exercises to perform, and other seemingly simple aspects of life that they must improve to reduce the symptoms of borderline personality disorder.

Self-Care

Some commonsensical self-care habits may, in fact, help improve the BPD condition. The patient must have good sleeping habits. Too much or too little sleep can contribute to both mental and physical health issues. They must manage stress to avoid any extreme reactions. They should also eat healthy foods because a healthy wellbeing also contributes to the mental and emotional wellbeing. They should not forget or skip medications as they are there to stabilize the condition. While they may not help but be suspicious or hurt at times, they must understand that his/her friends and family are working hard to provide them with proper treatment and support.

There are various treatments out there, but they are not really cures. One of the best treatments that a BPD sufferer can have is being with understandable and committed friends and family. Through this, they will see just how loved and wanted they really are.

Chapter 10:
Can you Overcome Borderline Personality Disorder?

According to specialists, borderline personality disorder or BPD is one of the most difficult mental illnesses to overcome. After all, it does combine a lot of the symptoms that we see in various related diseases. It is a condition wherein the sufferer can find it difficult to recognize the symptoms in themselves because they're not very willing communicators.

Why is it difficult to overcome BPD? BPD is a condition that presents as a different interpretation of emotions and other people's actions. Simple misunderstandings, without the help of BPD and other personality disorders, can cause so much trouble in people's lives. So, just imagine having these misunderstandings with someone who sees the world in a completely different way.

Imagine someone who also has a different sense of self, sometimes inflated and sometimes deflated. These extremes and viewing of world as black and white can really place the sufferer in a dark place. It separates them from family and friends because there is a divide in terms of emotional interpretation. In fact, some have gone as far as calling it "emotional dyslexia".

So, you are probably wondering now if your case is hopeless. It is difficult, yes, but nothing is really impossible when you try your best to overcome it. The first step would be to admit that you need help. You must first be able to recognize the troubling symptoms of borderline personality disorder.

If you have BPD, you are more than likely functioning well enough in society. This means to say that your family and friends are the ones who are suffering from the brunt of the condition. Let it then be your motivation to get better because you want to be able to mend and maintain your most intimate relationships.

Despite the difficulties presented by BPD, it is possible to overcome the condition. There have been sufferers who have successfully improved their behaviors and attitude, thus also improving their relationships and way of living. It can be done.

However, for this to happen, you must be able to humble yourself. You must accept that people who have approached you may be right about the possibility of you having a personality disorder. It can be next to impossible for an actual sufferer to consider the fact that they need help. However, when you have finally found the strength to recognize your symptoms, you have taken the first but most important step towards getting better.

You do have to commit yourself to whatever therapy or treatment your therapist decides to put you on. For everything to be successful, you will need an understanding therapist and supportive family and friends. Do understand, though, that you have to start things.

Chapter 11:
Self-Help Strategies

There are many self-help strategies for those with borderline personality disorder. In fact, when you attempt to get better from the condition, the first step is to help yourself. If others try to help you out but you are still unwilling, nothing will change. They will just end up frustrated, and you will end up severing important relationships. This chapter will introduce several self-help strategies that you may like to try.

Relaxation Techniques

In one of the previous chapters, relaxation techniques were mentioned. This is one of the more obvious self-help strategies. You do need to be able to calm yourself down. Why? BPD sufferers tend to court disaster by taking too many risks. Instead of taking a risk impulsively, try to stop a while and think about the possible repercussions. Do not just jump into the next big, exciting thing.

Take yoga or meditation classes. This way, you get to really stop for a while and tear yourself away from the usual stresses that life involves. If you practice yoga and meditation enough, you'll soon learn to relax yourself on command. Give yourself time to think and reflect, instead of just mouthing off or grabbing danger by the neck.

Stirring your imagination

Close your eyes and envision good things happening to you. Imagine things that will help you to relax. Perhaps you can work on something like imagining green grass and walking through it. Feel your feet touch the tips of the blades as you walk towards a clearing. Focus on the feelings, and all of the colors, sounds and smells in vivid detail. This will help you to relax, regroup, and clear your mind.

Mindfulness

The willingness to dissect the details of everyday life will help you take away some of your impulsive tendencies. It also helps you become a happier person, acknowledging whatever blessings – no matter how small – you have received. The fact that you were able to get up this morning should already be a triumph for you.

A great way to start is to make a list of everything that made you smile this week, or everything that you're thankful for. This is a great activity to try when you feel down or depressed.

Engaging in activities

There are activities that will take your mind off what you are feeling deep inside. It is not a direct solution, but it should not be called an escape, either. Finding useful and helpful activities, such as volunteering or acquiring a hobby, is not a waste. Once you start to enjoy the activities, you will find something to be joyful, hopeful or inspired about life.

Some activities that may not exactly inspire joyfulness but will take your mind off some of the things that trouble it are sports, gardening, cross-words, and puzzles of all sorts.

Remaining in the present

Upon discovery of your own health diagnosis, you will realize that your condition may have caused some cracks in your relationships. Do not take this to heart, although don't be remorseless, either. If your friends and family care enough, then they will understand that you are going through something difficult. You can apologize, but you do not have to dwell in the mistakes of the past. Think of the present, and try to make the most out of it. By dwelling in the past, you just take away the enjoyment of life.

Muscle relaxation and exercise

Involving the physical in your self-help strategies will also help you out. After all, it's likely that you carry a lot of tension in your body. By relaxing your muscles, you improve your sense of wellbeing while also improving your mood.

Exercise is muscle relaxation's more vigorous but equally healthy cousin. If you find yourself thinking or acting sluggishly, do not give in to it. Perform some exercises. Exercises will help you feel healthier, in mind and body. Exercise also triggers the release of hormones that make you feel a lot happier and energized about life.

An attitude of commitment

Though committing to something, such as a treatment, does not exactly exude self-help, it does present the most important contribution that you yourself can give to the goal of overcoming borderline personality disorder. With an attitude of commitment, you show that you are willing to go the distance. Even if friends, family, and your therapist are doing their utmost best to take you out of your rut, it is ultimately you that can really move things forward.

Mental and physical break

In today's society, we are all expected to perform a lot of jobs and wear many hats - sometimes all at the same time. The constant juggling and running can be taxing on anyone, even those with no personality disorders to contend with, so give yourself a few minutes' break when needed. Just sit down, away from all sorts of devices, and do nothing at all. Just sit there. Try to keep your mind blank as much as you can. You need this break. Allow yourself to relax and feel a sense of calmness.

Music therapy

You may have noticed that music can change your mood, so if you are feeling down, look for some music that can lift it up. Do not indulge the depressed feeling by listening to 'angsty' music. Listen to dance music as you exercise or listen to soothing music as you try to manage your anger.

It is difficult to think positive when you have borderline personality disorder. So, you have to take some of these things with a grain of salt. As you keep on doing what you have committed to do, you will feel some sense of accomplishment as well as some improvement.

Chapter 12:
Where to Go for Help/Diagnosis

Despite the availability of self-help strategies, every person is different. To really understand the severity of your condition, it is best to get checked. Self-diagnosis and self-prescription have never been a recommendation. Besides, with professional help, you can get correctly analyzed and have access to the required treatments. Do not lean towards experimentation.

Professional help

There are several directories online or otherwise that will show you the names and contact numbers of psychologists and psychiatrists in your area. You may want to call their numbers to find out if they treat borderline personality disorder specifically. Some may advertise themselves as behavioral therapists who do specialize in personality disorders. That will definitely help you zero in on a few names. You can try calling them up. If you have a good health insurance or a big enough budget for the checkups, then you may want to try at least two or three of the therapists to see which one makes you feel the most comfortable.

Support groups

You may also join support groups. The other members are also BPD sufferers. This will make it easier for you to understand which among your behaviors are considered normal and which are considered risky, impulsive or ultimately relationship wreckers. You will learn this from the members of the group that you have joined. By listening to the other stories, you will find hope and support in each other. Share your own tale about BPD. It is good to know that you are also helping others with this sharing.

Family and friends

Of course, some of the best people to run to are your family and friends. They are the ones who will best understand you. They will appreciate your efforts in trying to get better and thus improving your relationship with them. They may be worried, confused, and perhaps even afraid at first, so you may want to invite them to one of your appointments with your therapist. Maybe they also have some questions that they want to pose to your doctor.

By first going to a therapist, you become sure about your diagnosis. Take note that borderline personality disorder is difficult to diagnose even by experts, because of its similarities to other conditions, so it is definitely not wise to self-diagnose. You are not alone in your journey towards a better wellbeing, either. You can elicit the help of strangers with similar conditions and see how different or the same you all are. There may be success stories that can help give you hope.

Think about your family and friends who are trying their best to understand you and who would like to have a healthier relationship with you.

If, on the other hand, you are reading this for someone in your family or close circle of friends with BPD, have hope. Treatment can help the BPD sufferer feel better about themselves. Once they are ready and eager, they will be able to move closer to improving their understanding of what constitutes proper behavior. It will be a slow process, but they will improve, and your relationship with the person will strengthen and grow.

Conclusion

Thank you again for downloading this book!

I hope this book was able to help you learn more about borderline personality disorder!

The next step is to put this information to use, and begin managing and improving your borderline personality disorder! If you read this on the behalf of a loved one, please don't hesitate to talk to them about their condition. The sooner you take action to improve BPD, the sooner things will begin to improve.

Finally, if you enjoyed this book, please take the time to share your thoughts and post a review on Amazon. It'd be greatly appreciated!

Thank you and good luck!

www.ingramcontent.com/pod-product-compliance
Lightning Source LLC
LaVergne TN
LVHW021739060526
838200LV00052B/3370